Skinny
the Cat
and the
Magic
of Kindness

Skinny
the Cat
and the
Magic
of Kindness

Donna Rawlins

EPIGRAPH BOOKS
RHINEBECK NY

Printed in the United States of America

Book and Cover Design: Christina Renzi

Epigraph Books
22 East Market Street, Suite 304
Rhinebeck, NY 12572
www.epigraphPS.com
USA 845-876-4861

Printed in the United States of America.
ISBN: 978-1-936940-15-8 (hard cover)
ISBN: 978-1-936940-16-5 (soft cover)
Library of Congress Control Number: 2011938305

AUTHOR'S NOTE

All the cats in this story are rescue cats.

Some names and locations have been altered to protect privacy.

CONTENTS

ACKNOWLEDGEMENTS

Countless thanks to Deb Ondo of OndoCreative.com for all your grounding common sense, marketing expertise, and delightful pep talks. Also special thanks to Andy Lerner, Melody Feist, Harriet Rawlins Hill, and Kim Everhart for your skilled assistance, along with Emily Rawlins-Struckmann, Stacy and Dr. John Young, Beth Wernick, Lynn Martin, Tamara Fowler, my parents, Esther and Harry Rawlins; Dr. Roger Valentine, and all my other pet-loving family and friends for their emotional support and willingness to Get Skinnied!

INTRODUCTION

If someone told me ten years ago that a cat would teach me how to soften hardened hearts through the magic of kindness and I would be so moved by the experience I would publish a book about it, I'd have thought that was pretty funny. But the truth is, that's precisely what happened. A cat called Skinny, completely changed my life.

Observing the instinctive behavior—dare I say *insistence*—of this scrawny creature to never take no for an answer, to never give up in the face of rejection, and showing up on our doorstep again and again with the sweetest demeanor imaginable, was the catalyst for my epiphany about the transformative power—or magic—of kindness. It's easy to be nice to someone who is nice in return. But being *relentlessly* kind in the throes of prolonged admonition—while peacefully holding a position until a situation transforms—is another subject altogether, and what this little cat tale is all about.

We are taught to value kindness. Kindness commonly *begets* kindness and the effect of that goodwill generates a productive ripple through society. So being nice is ... *nice*. It makes other people feel good, plus, there is a tangible, personal joy in doing good deeds. But, speaking for myself, I never thought much about it beyond this basic understanding ... until I met Skinny.

At first sighting, I didn't know his name and because he was particularly thin, my husband and I defaulted to calling him Skinny. I assumed his slender physique was from an inadequate diet during his formerly blighted, pre-rescued life, though later, I discovered it was more likely a factor of his DNA, possibly of Siamese influence. As time passed however, his owner (our neighbor, Jan) "formally" introduced us, and I learned his real name was Floyd. But based on his comical personality, my husband and I couldn't relinquish our habit of referring to him as Skinny. As he gained a tiny bit of weight, we tried other nicknames like Thin and Thinster ... but Skinny is what stuck.

Inspired by his chronic persistence and ability to love at any price, he became my personal icon for peace. That, in conjunction with the impact he continues to have on animals, on me, and on other people, compelled me to give voice to his story. The more people who read about Skinny and are motivated in their own lives to emulate the actions of this peacekeeper, the more we can help spur the ripple effect of kindness through our social circles and on out into the world.Skinny reminds us that the very people (or animals, in some cases), needing our compassion and gentleness the most, appear to be the *least* deserving of it. So, in short, *Skinny the Cat and the Magic of Kindness* is about loving those who seem unlovable and watching your world change as a result.

It is my pleasure to present this story of a skinny little rescue cat: his ability to love in spite of continual rejection, his power to alter the dynamic of an entire neighborhood, and how Skinny's magic leaves an imprint on the souls it touches.

Though it's commonly accepted that humans are more highly evolved than our furry companions, they certainly have much to teach us ... if we let them.

No act of kindness,
no matter how small,
is ever wasted.

—Aesop, *"The Lion and the Mouse"*

Bhava

Chapter One

MEET BHAVA

Before Robert and I were married, Bhava lived as his housemate in Venice, California, about a mile from the notorious Muscle Beach. Although Bhava never made it down to the beach to work out, she definitely exhibited some muscle around the neighborhood. She was unapproachable by most other felines and seemed to fancy herself as the queen of her domain, the alpha female of Clement Avenue.

Perhaps some of her fiery personality traits came from her rough start. Robert's friend, Jana, was out in her garden near Palm Springs one day when, in the heat of the Mojave Desert, a tiny kitten not more than six weeks old staggered out from beneath a nearby bush and then collapsed at her feet. The poor little thing was parched and starving and so thin that her ribs were easily seen through dusty black-and-white fur.

After Jana restored this frail animal back to health, she packed her up and drove straight to Robert's, hoping the element of surprise would diminish his resistance to her impromptu attempt at adoption. So tiny she could stand in the palm of Robert's hand, the still-nameless kitten climbed up his shirtsleeve and careened around his shoulders to rub her head on his ear, which made him laugh. *But Robert didn't want a cat.* After he told Jana he honestly wasn't the right person for the job, she reluctantly retrieved the curious pint-sized mewer and, with a heavy sigh, said, "Well ... I guess you can't save *every* life," intimating a trip to the shelter. Well, that was it. Game over.

Being a yoga enthusiast, Robert settled on the Sanskrit name Bhava and quickly adapted to her, as her ability to make him smile grew with every passing day. Kittens are good at that.

Often, while Robert watered the roses that lined the front edge of his cozy two-bedroom house, a male cat named Sebastian from across the street would wander over to do a ritualistic once-around through Robert's legs and then hop onto the porch to peer through the screen door, attempting to get a peek at Bhava inside the house. He'd rub his cheek on the corners of the doorway and then flop down, belly up on the cement, inviting a vigorous tummy rub. I thought it all completely innocent and adorable, until one fateful Saturday when Bhava came home with much more than a black eye.

As Robert cleaned up the breakfast dishes, the unsettling screeches of a catfight shot through the kitchen window. Recalling that Bhava was still outside enjoying her morning walk and could possibly be involved, Robert raced into the street, unhappily confirming that something ugly had indeed transpired.

Drool dripped lavishly from the mouths of the two cats as they squared off for yet another round. Sebastian, obviously vying for the dominant alpha spot, hissed wickedly and stared into the squinted eyes of the last feline in his way: Bhava. Based on Sebastian's ruffled appearance, it seemed she had held her own and thrown some down and dirty punches, but reality quickly set in as Robert noted her drooping eyelid and dazed expression. She had finally met her match. Retrieving his bruised and bleeding little darling, he and Bhava headed straight for the veterinarian.

We were shocked to learn the truth about Sebastian. (Just when you think you really know your neighbors!) I did learn from this experience that in addition to the deceptive coyness of some cats in the feline kingdom, there is neither respect for the female gender, nor an assumption they are necessarily the weaker sex. It's every cat for himself or herself, and gender has no clear bearing on social order.

Back home with patched-up wounds and (ouch) a torn inner eyelid, Bhava truly had seen better days. To fend off a potential abscess, Robert faced the enormous task of administering not only eyedrops, but also an antibiotic liquid by mouth twice a day—in my opinion, a job only one step down in intensity from the nearly impossible chore of giving a cat a bath.

A typical bachelor-style Saturday afternoon included running errands, catching up with laundry, and general household duties. In contrast to the drama of this particular morning, it was a relief for Robert to focus on these otherwise tedious tasks. After loading freshly washed clothes into the dryer and retiring to the back of the house to pay a few bills, Robert couldn't help but notice an odd thumping sound coming from the laundry room. Initially dismissing it as a twisted pair of blue jeans that would shortly un-wad themselves, he sat down at his desk to sort through the mail, but ... the thumping continued. Returning to investigate what was making such a racket, he opened the dryer door and to his horror a very hot and stunned Bhava limply fell into his arms. Instantly snapping out of her stupor, she took a nosedive to the floor and ran as fast as she could to find refuge under the nearest bed.

Good grief. She had used up two of her nine lives in just one day, and it wasn't even dusk yet. Needless to say, Bhava was in a very bad mood. She refused to emerge from under the bed; this battle with Sebastian triggered two observable, posttraumatic conclusions: *nobody* was going to bully Ms. Bhava, and other cats were not to be trusted ... or liked.

ICHI

Chapter Two

BHAVA MEETS ICHI

Although I grew up with and love dogs, as an adult I became attracted to the feline kingdom—initially because of their legendary self-sufficiency. One could leave a cat for the weekend with a big bowl of dry food, some fresh water, and a clean litter box. That's even easier than fish. However, I soon realized cats are also *teachers*.

A proud Maine Coon with long, silky gray fur, a pink nose, and black lips, Ichi was my first cat as well as my spiritual guru. During our initial lessons together, he taught me not only patience but also the vast differences between cats and dogs. *Outside*, he enjoyed relaxing on top of the neighbors' rickety fence while their German shepherd jumped up and down barking furiously, intent on having kitty tartare for dinner. *Inside* the house, Ichi discovered the ceiling by climbing up the curtains—while I, in response, perfected the art of climbing the walls. After the first nail-biting twenty-four hours, I was more than ready to return him, but my friend who had personally rescued Ichi out of a North Hollywood alley talked me into giving him another try.

As time went on, he became as endearing to me as he was a good sport, and we continued to develop a light-hearted relationship. I had no children, so he assumed the positions of firstborn, tolerant friend, and steadfast companion. Before I met Robert, when I was navigating through the challenges of a new career, the cat and I transitioned to the west side of Los Angeles and moved into the sweetest and tiniest apartment in Santa Monica. Ichi often lay on my bed at night watching me sleep, as if I were the queen of the world and he, my furry gray prince. But in the wee hours of the morning, he had a habit of waking me by gently placing his paw on my cheek. If my eyes refused to open at his bidding, he tried again, lightly pushing the tips of his needle-like claws into my sleepy skin. In exchange for his tender torture tactics, I'd get back by teasing him with pre-meal antics requesting that he sing for his supper with a chorus of mews, as even the slightest delay in receiving his food brought out the familial lion in him, which I found deliriously amusing.

And when that cat walked out the front door, he definitely commanded respect. With his tail held high in the air and a confident strut, he would pause at the edge of the porch for a brief assessment of the neighborhood. Then, with one robust flick of the tail, off he'd go to relieve himself in the garden to freshen up the pheromones and reinforce his domain. Driven by his confident nature, he refused to cover up his excrements, yet conversely, in an odd exhibition of ancestral heritage, he went through the motions of concealing his *food* and would repeatedly paw the hardwood floor around his bowl after meals, even if only a small morsel was left.

Another quirk in his personality was his desire to run in and out of the apartment. To make it easier on both of us, I secured an opening in the living-room window just big enough for him to slither through to gain access to his custom-built terrace—a window-high platform supported by the sycamore tree a few feet away, which had been ingeniously constructed by my thoughtful neighbors, Ian and Donalie.

One night, I awakened to the sound of munching. Assuming Ichi was up having a late-night snack, I didn't think too much about it. Unable to get back to sleep and slightly annoyed by the kibble crunching, I opened my eyes, ready to demand that he stop eating (as if one has that much control over a cat). Much to my surprise, Ichi was lying a few feet from his bowl, watching a baby opossum scarf down the rest of his chow. He was as calm as if he was watching an interesting episode of Marlin Perkins's *Wild Kingdom*. My heart, on the other hand, was doing its imitation of a jack-hammer. I was horrified that an undomesticated creature, especially one that looked like a giant rat, had invaded my apartment. Eventually I did get the so-ugly-he's-cute critter safely back outside by setting up a maze of cardboard boxes that guided the opossum back through the window from whence he came. However, in light of Ichi's apparent interest in other animals, I decided it wasn't such a good idea to leave the window open at night, in spite of his nocturnal roaming instincts. For me, it completely redefined the expression *look what the cat dragged in.*

Finally, our wedding day arrived. In the backyard of Robert's humble Clement Avenue home, we were surrounded by gorgeous white flowers, family, and friends, and our ceremony under the orange tree was about to be absolutely perfect. It was a gentle first day of autumn in southern California, with the sun high in the sky and not a cloud in sight. To me, everything was right with the world. Bhava, on the other hand, had a much different perspective. Being around more than one or two people at a time was pure torture for her, so to have the entire backyard filled with humans she didn't even know was nothing less than horrifying, especially right in the middle of afternoon naptime. And as you might anticipate, Bhava had ways of letting us know how she felt about this disruption in her day.

Just before the ceremony, when emotions were running high, she skillfully inched her way into the dining room unnoticed, where a beautiful yet untouched spread of appetizers were artfully arranged around the three-tier wedding cake. As we tended to last-minute adjustments in the kitchen, Bhava, being a master of waiting until your

BHAVA

attention is elsewhere, seized the moment and seamlessly jumped onto the table for a sample of wedding cake icing.

Of course, I can't be sure if it was solely in retaliation for wreaking havoc on her normally peaceful afternoon, her lust for the forbidden, or simply her uncontrollable desire for sweets, but in order to minimize the "inconvenience" of our wedding, we placed Bhava in a specially made fluffy bed in the office and shut the door ... tight. My friend Beth agreed to look in on her as the afternoon progressed, so we could enjoy this auspicious occasion without further concern.

In contrast to Bhava, Ichi loved having people over, so the wedding wasn't a problem for him at all. Ichi was mixing well, darting in and out of the house discovering all the wonderful new hiding places under the white linen cloths draped over the rented tables in the backyard. As for Ms. Bhava, she did her best to deafen the sounds of the frivolities by falling into a deep slumber, hoping when she awoke all the people would be gone.

With the wedding and honeymoon behind us, we were now officially a family. Historically, Ichi was flexible and never minded moving to a new home ... well, until this part of the story. Because Robert and I skipped the live-together-before-marriage option and combined our households a mere fifteen days prior to the wedding, the feline portion of that move was considerably less romantic. During those first two weeks, due to their countless adjustment squabbles, there was enough fur lost to stuff a few pillows. We would come home on any given day only to find wads of gray fur (his) and black fur (hers) randomly scattered throughout the house.

BHAVA AND ICHI

Ichi and Bhava

Bhava enjoyed baiting her new roommate with disarming antics, teasing him with pseudo-friendly gestures like rolling over on her back, pretending to initiate play. I must say it didn't take Ichi long to catch on to her warring tactics, but then again, it doesn't take too many clawed paw-punches to convince anyone to be wary of a territorial feline. After fighting furiously for their terrain, Ichi evolved into the kitchen cat and Bhava became known as the bedroom cat.

A few months later, we moved our little family to a bigger home. Since Ichi did not have the same fighting issues as Bhava, once we settled in he refused to grapple with her and, consistent with his peaceful personality, simply let her have her way. As a result of his nonviolent demeanor, he also enjoyed the extra privilege of lying in his favorite spot underneath the lavender bush in the front garden.

At sixteen years old, he was clearly the elder of our particular cat community and went about his business, watching the neighborhood from under the lavender bush or atop the white stucco wall on the front porch, and, of course, reminding me twice daily when it was time to eat. He actually got so fat we often worried he might cease to fit through the cat door in the back. Fortunately and unfortunately, that never happened.

Floyd (aka Skinny) and Romeo

Chapter Three

THE INVASION OF FLOYD (AKA SKINNY) AND BROTHER ROMEO

Robert and I were curious about the two unfamiliar cats that had been hanging around our new house. Little did we know at that time, our lives were about to be changed forever.

Long, lean, and inseparable, the lively duo began their quest of taking over the neighborhood. Both were beautifully marked cats. Romeo was long, dark, and handsome. He didn't say too much but was clearly the enforcer—the muscle of the two and the ringleader of the soon-to-be-formed Beach Avenue Cat Gang, aka the BACG. His brother, Floyd, was the lover. A shorthaired, gray gazelle-looking cat with big ears and a passionate Siamese cry, he was clearly the spokescat for the two of them. Both were rescue kittens and Floyd in particular was barely skin, bones, and fur when we first encountered him. I admit our perspective might have been a bit skewed since we were more accustomed to slightly fat cats like Ichi, but Floyd was truly the skinniest cat we'd met in a long time. So, after a few weeks we simply referred to him as Skinny. The nickname stuck. His extra-long body and lengthy tail accentuated his slim physique, making him look quite amusing. But that cat could jump over a fence as gracefully as any animal we'd ever seen. And as time went on, we were as impressed with his persistence as we were with his agility. Although he was skittish around human beings and impossible to physically touch, he wanted to be on the inside of our house—and our lives. Brother Romeo liked us, but Skinny, for whatever reasons, *loved* us and did anything possible to penetrate the security of our backyard.

We tried to create a safe haven for both Ichi and Bhava by adding lattice to the top of the existing fence in the backyard to increase the height from six to eight feet. We felt confident this adequately deterred feral cats and other animals from intruding, while at the same time prevented our little lovelies from getting out and illicitly roaming the neighborhood. Robert also installed a kitty door to keep the woodsy atmosphere and fresh air available to them at all times. Having 24-7 outdoor access also kept litter-box cleaning down to a minimum—a side benefit I was pleased about.

At this point, we assumed the backyard was secure. Therefore, I was understandably shocked the day I returned home from running errands to find Skinny inside our house. As soon as he laid eyes on me, he scampered in circles around the dining-room table, buying some time to think up an escape route after being caught in the act. Meanwhile, Ichi lay in his usual sphinx position a few feet away, calmly watching the rogue fugitive. I opened the front door and zoom ... out he ran. I could not for the life of me figure out how Skinny outsmarted our cat-proof security system.

Then, one afternoon a few weeks later, the truth finally came out when I caught Skinny off-guard, sneaking around the backyard again. In his haste to leave, he inadvertently revealed his path. I couldn't contain my laughter as I watched this long, scrawny cat retrace his steps, frantically scrambling up our orange tree and then clambering off into the neighboring yard.

Ah-ha! I had figured it out. To get into our yard,

he'd first take an easy hop onto the hood—and then to the roof—of the car belonging to our next-door neighbor. Crouched and furiously wiggling his tail end, he would make a judicious leap upward and land on the roof of the adjacent shed, where he gained access to the narrow top edge of our fence. Poised for his next major feat, Skinny balanced his long, thin body on the half-inch-wide lattice with the grace of a seasoned tightrope walker. Tilting to the left, to the right, and back to the left again, he'd dig his claws into the soft wood to sustain his balance, and then with acrobatic precision, dive into the top branches of our orange tree. At this point, it was a simple climb down. *Voila!* Mission accomplished.

Once we understood how he was getting in, we clearly needed to strengthen our defensive position. Staying out was not at all on Skinny's agenda, so it was time for us to get creative and not worry too much about how it looked to the neighbors. We scanned the garage for something we could weave into the tree branches to block his way into our yard, but all we found was a discarded, extra-large aluminum mini-blind. So up went Robert into the orange tree, ladder and rope in tow. I have to hand it to him. He did an effective job of splaying out the blind in a way that thereafter kept Skinny out of our backyard. Fortunately, it did not keep him out of our hearts.

I CHI

Chapter Four

SAYING GOOD-BYE TO ICHI

Robert and I were preparing to leave for a long-awaited vacation to Hawaii. We hadn't been on a real holiday for almost five years. For the past six weeks, I had planned carefully, organizing every detail so our two nights in Waikiki and five nights at Hanalei Bay, Kauai, would be perfect. Rest, relax, surf, snorkel, eat, drink, and be merry.

I arranged for Beth to take care of the beasts. I worried about Ichi, though, who for the past year had been battling a failing renal condition and had lost an astonishing amount of weight. If it weren't for the extraordinary expertise of our holistic vet, Dr. Valentine, we're certain Ichi would have been gone a year prior. Consequently, there was a three-page care list just for Ichi. Beth was a saint for offering to cat-sit. The particulars of his care, when actually committed to paper, seemed almost ridiculously meticulous, and yet, without this specialized treatment, we feared he might not make it through the vacation without us. In his prime, Ichi was a good-sized cat of thirteen pounds, but his little body was deteriorating in spite of the fact he was still full of life and spirit.

I have a tendency to keep a full schedule and long to-do lists no matter what is going on in my life, so it stands to reason this particular Saturday morning I crammed too many things to do in a time frame not quite big enough. I thought I had all the details of closing up the house for a week arranged down to the minute and had included the twenty to thirty minutes we'd have to wait for the cab to take us to the airport.

With bags packed, trash taken out, and breakfast eaten, it was time for Robert to call the cab, which, according to my calculations, gave me at least twenty minutes to finish my coffee, load the dishes in the dishwasher, run upstairs to brush my teeth, take one last look at the feline care instructions to make sure I hadn't forgotten anything, and say good-bye to our furry friends. Easy.

Well, just as I checked off the dishwasher task, the cab arrived. This couldn't be. It had only been ten minutes since he called. I hadn't brushed my teeth, gone over the list, or said *adieu* to Ichi and Bhava. We planned to be gone for an entire week, and I needed a few loving moments with each of them to make sure they understood we were only going on vacation and Auntie Beth would be coming over twice a day to give them all the love and care they needed and that we'd be home soon ... that it was only seven sunrises and seven sunsets—you know, all the little, but important, neurotic things pet owners do.

There just wasn't enough time, so out the door we flew, blowing kisses to the kitties and accepting the fact I'd have to brush my teeth at the airport and call Beth later to double check the list. Okay. That would have to work.

And indeed, everything went well. The vacation was fabulous, Beth checked in with us every day so we didn't have to worry, and life was wonderful.

We arrived home one week and a day later at 6:00 am on Sunday, exhausted from the night flight but refreshed from the break away from our routine. We walked into the house desperate for a furry-cat fix. Bhava was there to greet us at the door, but Ichi was nowhere to be found. We looked in all the usual hideaways: the downstairs linen closet, the office closet, behind the computer, and under the desk. Still ... no Ichi. We combed the rest of the house, examining each and every closet and drawer. We looked under every bush and plant in both the front and back yards, even though there was no logical way he could have gotten out of the backyard. We were in the middle of a true nightmare. Reality was setting in. In spite of the fact he was there the night before when Beth fed him at 7:30, Ichi was gone.

Twenty-three long, *long* hours passed. Exhausted from restless, shallow sleep, we still crawled out of bed at five with the orange sky and cresting morning sun to light the way. Robert dressed and hit the streets with his instincts on high. Trusting his intuition and insisting that Ichi was nearby and still alive, he refused to give up on finding my little gray prince. I was so distraught that I was no help at all and sat motionless, crying on the front steps of our house, waiting for Robert's return and any news about Ichi. With each inhale, I exhaled more paralyzing tears of grief.

In the past, when Ichi was healthy and loved to eat, Robert had trained him to come to the sound of a can of cat food being shaken inside a small Tupperware container. Having learned the delicious reward, Ichi couldn't resist the tempting sound and predictably came running out of any remote hiding place if he was in reasonable earshot of that dinner rattle. The first day of our search, however, Robert's attempts to draw him out of seclusion in this way proved to be fruitless. He paced up and down every street in the neighborhood, systematically calling Ichi's name while tirelessly shaking the little can of stinky cat food that toggled inside the plastic container. Every few houses, he paused to listen intently and sharpen his mental focus on our lost cat, trying to sense or intuit where he might be.

I'm not sure what was different the second morning. Perhaps it was Robert's renewed determination to find him or possibly an angel whispered to him in the night, but this time he went out to the streets with a specific hunch about where to look and was absolutely right. Just one street over, Ichi suddenly staggered out of the brush from a neighbor's yard. He was barely able to walk and badly dehydrated because of lack of fluids and his severe kidney condition. Thankfully he couldn't resist the food instinct—and thankfully, Robert was unyielding in his attempts to find him. Otherwise, we never would have known what happened.

Robert came running down the middle of the street yelling to me, "I've got him! I've got him! He's alive!" Barely believing my ears, I jumped up from the front porch stairs and ran into the street to meet them. It was true. There was Robert running toward me with little Ichi tightly held in his arms, bouncing lightly from the rhythm of his trot. I barely even noticed the tears standing in Robert's eyes as I smothered my little man in joyful kisses.

When he was safe inside, Ichi ate ravenously, and luckily, we had supplies to hydrate him subcutaneously. Unfortunately, our vet was out of the country, but that afternoon one of his colleagues was able to make a house call. She gave Ichi some B12 and Chinese herbs. He was down to 6.2 pounds. For a formerly thirteen-pound cat, this was not good news.

In retrospect, we calculated that at that small weight, he must have been slender enough to slip through the three-inch opening alongside the back gate leading into the alley. Like most sick animals, he instinctively knew nature was reclaiming him—that it was his time to die. Perhaps somewhere in the kindness of his cat soul, he wanted to spare us from watching him go and went into the wild to peacefully pass alone.

We kept him alive for ten more days. Unable to overcome the wrath of renal failure, perhaps we should have let him go earlier, but ... letting go is never easy. He was family. He was my kid. After spending countless hours holding him, singing to him, and praying for guidance, we made the most gut-wrenching decision a pet owner ever faces: to let him pass. In Dr. Valentine's absence, one of our friends, also a veterinarian, came to our home to compassionately help Ichi along on his journey.

Three days prior to that ill-fated day, I had abruptly awakened from a dream in which an angel calling herself Kayah appeared to me. Dressed in a flowing gown of white gauze, a silent breeze tossed the skirt of her dress and her blond tendrils about aimlessly, as she looked at me with the most caring blue eyes I had ever seen. She explained she was waiting for Ichi. That she was the one who would receive him in the other dimension and would take care of him during his passing. I needn't worry. She extended her right arm, pointing as if showing me a direction ... to *where* I did not know, but I knew it was serene and lovely. Extending from her long fingers was a glowing beam of intense white light illuminating a grassy path through a fragrant meadow. She looked at me and smiled, saying, "He'll be safe with me. I promise."

In my opinion, it's impossible to fully express the grief of losing a close animal companion, no matter what you believe or don't believe happens after physical death. And even my dream—as comforting as it should have been— did not dilute the intense ache of his not being around. Of course, it diminished over time, but in the weeks that followed Ichi's death, there didn't seem to be a moment I wasn't twirling a thought of him around in my mind, nor a day or a night I didn't deeply long for his presence back in my physical world. Sometimes, the feelings were so great that I thought my heart would surely explode. At other times, in a rare moment of not thinking about my dearly departed friend, I'd unexpectedly catch sight of him out of the corner of my eye ... only to turn to see his absence.

SKINNY AT OUR FRONT DOOR

Chapter Five

DEEPENING THE RELATIONSHIP

Skinny's persistence did not wane, and again, I found myself in awe of the mystical nature of cats. He seemed to sense the void in our hearts. No one could take Ichi's place, but it was interesting to observe Skinny's sixth sense in knowing Robert and I needed extra love, which he graciously gave to us with curious bashfulness, making him even more endearing.

Luckily, he was getting fatter, ny wasn't so skinny anymore and was growing into a remarkable creature. He'd hang around the front door—sometimes by himself, sometimes with his brother, Romeo—and it seemed he never wanted to leave. Often, I saw his silhouette in the opaque glass door panel, with the western sun backlighting his body and oversized ears. It hauntingly reminded me of Ichi when he stood in that exact spot patiently waiting to come back into the house, smelling sweetly of lavender after his afternoon sunbath in the garden.

As time went on, the two young cat brothers, Skinny and Romeo, entertained each other as Bhava grumpily observed them from the windows of our two-story house. The floor-to-ceiling window in the downstairs dining room enabled her to sit on the floor and silently stare out the bottom pane—her bright yellow eyes peering through the glass. Our upstairs bedroom, however, was the ultimate spy tower. A built-in set of cabinet drawers alongside a window with a twenty-five-foot purple-flowered jacaranda tree a few feet away provided the perfect vantage point to enjoy close-ups

BHAVA SCRUTINIZING THE BACG

of birds flying by, resting in the trees, or playing on the red Mexican tiles on the roof over the porch just below. With this magnificent view of the neighborhood, she was able to keep a close eye on everything.

Among her visual targets were Skinny and Romeo playing chicken with the fat crows and running after each other, flying over fences and chasing each other through the neighbors' lawns, until one day when we noticed they weren't just chasing each *other* anymore. A new cat had

appeared on the scene. It seemed to the human eye that this particular cat stranger was unceasingly harassed and pursued by the Beach Avenue Cat Gang, (the BACG): Romeo and Skinny. Even though I assumed this was part of the natural feline hazing ritual for cat gangs, I scolded them for chasing that anonymous black cat. I later learned human eyes do not always interpret the animal kingdom as accurately as we would like to think.

SKINNY AND HIS NEW FRIEND, SASHA

Chapter Six

SKINNY ADOPTS SASHA

We asked around the neighborhood, but no one knew where the unidentified black cat had come from. Was she an aimless refugee, an unwanted drop-off, or perhaps a runaway? She was certainly adorable, demure, and strong-willed. That much I knew. It took weeks of coaxing before I finally got close enough to see what was written on the shiny blue tag attached to her frayed collar. On one side it read Sasha and on the other side was the disconnected phone number of her former owner.

One morning as I was finishing my daily walk, I noticed Jan working in her garden, and I decided to stop by to compare notes. According to Jan, Sasha was showing up for dinner every night, and Skinny insisted not only that she eat—but also that she eat first. He seemed to have adopted Sasha and literally stepped aside at feeding time so she could dine ahead of him. I'd never heard of such a polite cat.

So the question became this: How did Sasha go from being chased by the boys to being invited over for dinner? Had she held her own through the hazing process and earned herself a spot in the BACG? Or had Skinny been trailing her with the pure intention of welcoming her into the neighborhood? We are now convinced it was the latter, but either way, Sasha somehow earned her spot at the food dish, Jan had another mouth to feed, and Skinny had a new friend. Sasha was officially one of the gang.

We watched as the three of them continued to romp through yards and cavort around the neighborhood. They seemed to favor resting on our front porch bench, and we frequently found them there catnapping, each curled up into a little ball. And as the cats grew closer to each other, we grew closer to them. It quickly became a ritual to anticipate their visits and for me to make sure there were old towels or a blanket available for them to sleep on.

As comfortable summer and fall breezes transformed into the chill of approaching southern California winter rains, we were understandably concerned about the outdoor trio. The BACG was still intact and spending increasingly more time on our front porch—so much time, in fact, I had several conversations with Jan just to assure her I was not attempting to kidnap her cats.

Once the January sprinkles started, the blankets and towels were moved from the light-green bench to just outside the front door under the protection of the overhang, where we built a makeshift cat camp to shield them from the damp weather. We took a long cardboard box that was big enough for the three of them, padded the bottom with newspaper, and laid Skinny's favorite dark-green blanket on top of the newspaper. In an effort to make their shelter look less unsightly, I dug through my old linens, ran across a retired white shower curtain, and laid that on top of the box, attempting to camouflage the (if you will) *cat* house so it blended in better with the surrounding white stucco walls of the people house. It worked fairly well and the cats certainly enjoyed their new hut. Everybody was happy, and I was having lots of fun playing feline den mother.

One drizzly Saturday morning, Robert and I walked outside to find Sasha solo, snoozing the morning away in the white-and-green hut. The boys had gone out early, perhaps to get a little exercise. She was such a cutie and looked even more adorable half awake in the new digs. We cooed and mewed, kissed her on the top of the head, and left to get some breakfast down by the beach. The extra rain had stirred the

ROMEO, SKINNY, AND SASHA

ocean, and reports indicated the waves measured over ten feet. We couldn't resist the opportunity to gaze at the not-so-blue-anymore Pacific Ocean.

As we approached home after our morning outing an hour or so later, something on the side of the street in front of our house caught my attention. I squinted, trying to decipher if it was a fallen tree branch or perhaps a small jacket someone dropped on his or her morning walk. As we drew closer, I realized it was nothing of the sort. It was a cat ... a black cat. My heart raced and breath refused to escape my lips. Stunned and horrified, I frantically hurried out of the car to take a closer look. I leaned down, touched the deathly still, soft, furry body. Insanely calm and in complete denial, I looked at Robert and emphatically informed him it was not Sasha. I didn't know whose cat it was, but it definitely was not Sasha. Over and over, I repeated the declaration like a mantra while Robert heartbreakingly tried to help me clear my thoughts and realize the truth of what had actually happened. I screamed. I cried. I refused to believe the reality until, through my tears, as I held her lifeless body in my shaking arms, I started to see the identifying scanty ring of white fur around the top of her neck. It was true. As difficult as it was to understand, Sasha was gone. How had this sweet and gentle creature been suddenly ripped from our lives?

As we turned our attention to the scene of this horrible transgression, we observed deep pockmarks in the soft dirt alongside tufts of wet grass strewn about the lawn. They were clearly the footprints of a large dog. This, in addition to the overturned planters lining the edges of our porch and copious wads of dog hairs enmeshed in the damp cement, revealed it was not a car that hit and killed Sasha, as I first suspected. As we examined her petite corpse and discovered the bite wound on her back right side, it became conclusive that an unleashed dog had claimed her. I held her in my arms and wept, retracing my morning, wishing I had not been interested in the stupid waves. If I had only been here, perhaps I could have prevented the violence. Robert and I were both inconsolable. It was surreal. This simply could not have happened … but it had.

Jan was gone. We waited. We cried some more. We talked about our sadness and questioned the responsibility in this unspeakable act. We couldn't blame the dog for following its instinct to chase and kill a cat. But in the city of Los Angeles, not having your dog on a leash was and is against the law, and this crime was the result of an irresponsible owner. Did that change anything, though? Sasha was still dead in my arms, and there wasn't anything anyone could do to bring her back.

When Jan arrived, she mournfully took Sasha's stiffening body and laid her to rest in her backyard. We all agreed that the hut should be put away and the boys retrained to sleep at their house where Jan had already set up a safe sanctuary for them.

All of us were deeply and dramatically affected by this tragedy. It took Bhava nearly a week before she dared go near the window where she most assuredly watched the fateful incident. Skinny was not to be found on our property for days. Romeo wouldn't even walk past the gate and up onto our porch for weeks. Yes, Sasha would always be missed, and for months afterward, we felt her spirit among us.

SKINNY TIRELESSLY WAITING
ON OUR DOORSTEP

Chapter Seven

NEVER GIVE UP

No matter what happens in life, time moves us forward. After a few emotionally painful weeks, we reluctantly adapted to a new sense of normalcy. Skinny was more determined than ever to win over the indoor princess, Bhava. He rekindled his friendly courtship with frequent visits, sitting outside the front door waiting for an opportunity to say hello to her. When he wasn't waiting on the doormat, he assumed his perch on the arm of the light-green bench, staring into our living room, hoping perhaps to get a glimpse of her sleeping on the bed we had placed near the foot of the couch.

Skinny was famous for coming up to the door and then running away when one of us tried to pet him. Clearly, he needed love and wanted to give love, but he didn't quite have the hang of it yet—well, at least on human terms. After a multitude of attempts, we finally got through to him that it was not necessary to instantly jump out of someone's arms if picked up and embraced. He tolerated increasingly more petting and eventually relaxed enough to purr while being held.

As his comfort level increased, Skinny tried to sneak into the house any time we opened the front door. Bhava, also notorious for her tendency of breaking and entering (or exiting, as the case may be), never missed an opportunity to seamlessly fly out the door if left unwatched, even for a moment.

The inevitable presented itself one afternoon when both cats decided to simultaneously escape into each other's world. Mid-move, the magnetism of the two escapees

SKINNY LOOKING INTO
OUR LIVING ROOM

inspired a weighted pause at the doorway. Skinny took advantage of this opportune moment and did the curiously feline thing: He attempted to sniff Bhava's nose—something no cat had ever had the courage to do. From Bhava's perspective, clearly the prospect of another cat trying to get even remotely close, triggered her defense mechanisms.

Bam, bam, bam! With ears back and full-throttle power, Bhava smacked him right on top of his little gray head with a triple right paw punch. With absolutely no tolerance for this kind of aberrant behavior (gentle nose sniffing), she continued to pound on him until I pulled her away. No actual harm was done, but I did feel a bit embarrassed. I later had a chat with Skinny, explaining Bhava's lack of social skills and that perhaps it would be better if he just accepted the fact he needed to stay on the other side of the door. It was clear Bhava's intolerance for other animals had not changed one iota.

Ironically, it seemed that the more unlovable Bhava was, the more Skinny wanted to love her. It seemed nothing could dissuade him from continuing his attempts to befriend her.

Then, one afternoon, I was working in my upstairs office when I heard an unusually quick thumping sound. Uh-oh. That *bam, bam, bam* sounded frightfully familiar. I dashed down the carpeted stairs, noisily landing on the hardwood floor as I entered the living room. Unmoved by my strident entrance, there was Bhava, paw-punching the window with Romeo mirroring her swings in self-defense from the other side of the glass.

It turns out that Romeo stopped by to check out the feisty tuxedo princess but, as you might imagine, she didn't respond well to his peering through the window and made her opinion about that very clear. After this initial episode, I kept the curtains closed during the day to lessen her exposure to the stress. Unfortunately, this did nothing to end the window spats. For hours on end, Bhava secretly stood guard on the inside of the curtain, lying in wait for Romeo to appear, prepared for battle at any given moment that she wasn't busy snacking or napping. I knew we were in serious trouble the day I saw Bhava chewing furiously on the bottom edge of the curtain, eyes fixed in a mad frenzy, drooling onto the hardwood floor in mere anticipation of the next fight.

Oddly enough, none of this seemed to bother Skinny. He made no apologies for his brother's behavior and still came to the door, waiting to see if he could get another chance with the princess. But whenever she saw Skinny waiting on the other side of the door, she'd make a mad dash for the opening and stick her nose out just beyond the threshold in a baiting attempt to get close enough to pound him yet one more time.

Then one day, an astounding event occurred. Skinny was waiting just outside our front door as usual, and Bhava—always a move ahead of me—sneaked by and poked her head through the opening in the doorway, certainly anticipating Skinny would be there. But before she had a chance to pound on him, he managed to hold her attention just long enough for her to drop her defenses. And in this propitious moment, he rubbed the side of his head over her unsuspecting cheek. (Yes, you read that correctly.) So there they were, face-to-face, whisker-to-whisker.

Aghast, she jerked her head back. But surprisingly, this time she didn't retaliate by throwing punches. Amazed, I stood motionless and watched what happened next. I know it seems impossible to believe, but it's true. Head back with one paw two inches off the floor, cocked and ready to fight, she paused. After surveying the situation, she put her little foot back down on the floor, and then ... did something no one could have predicted: She actually leaned into him, bashfully rubbing her cheek on his.

But, as if she suddenly realized the implications of what she'd just done, she turned and made a beeline to the comfort zone of our hallway, where she stopped dead in her tracks and took a seat. Skinny stood in the doorway, proud of his triumph and, looking up at me with his big innocent eyes, seeming to ask, "Okay, so can I come inside now?"

Chuckling to myself, I realized that Bhava had just gotten "skinnied." His persistence had finally broken through the hard exterior of Bhava's heart, and I learned an unforgettable lesson that day: If kind gestures of friendship and harmony are steadfast, with time, patience, and perseverance, one can actually hope to see a smile on the face of even the most hardened curmudgeon.

Skinny Attempting to
Say Hello to Bhava

SKINNY

ROMEO

Chapter Eight

RECONCILIATION

Word got around fast. Skinny, along with his brother Romeo, showed up every day at the door. Skinny had apparently informed Romeo of Bhava's softening and seemed to be scheming to get all three of them together. Considering their prior relationship disputes and Bhava's curtain biting, I thought this was an extremely bold endeavor for Skinny to pursue. But I had to consider the source and his history of persistence. Still, I was reluctant to let her get near the front door for fear of a claw-to-claw battle with Romeo, but I must confess, I was curious about what might happen with Skinny at the helm.

Interestingly enough, as the days rolled by, we continued to observe Bhava's acceptance of Skinny and, yes, even Romeo. In that astonishing moment of surrender, something transformational had happened to her, and apparently any remaining animosities were now dissolved. It seemed that the ice princess finally warmed up to a concept that historically had evaded her: love and tolerance for her fellow felines. She realized there was no DNA-infused requirement to chronically defend herself against gestures of kindness or to automatically refuse love when it showed up on her doorstep.

A few days later when I opened the front door, Skinny was predictably waiting with his brother, Romeo, on the welcome mat. Not having a strict eye on Bhava in that particular instant, I was unaware of her close proximity to the escape hatch. I felt the ankle breeze as she bolted for the door. But just as the wind during a storm sometimes abruptly ceases to blow, there was a sudden silence.

I looked down and witnessed one of the most touching moments of my life. Three little cat noses were sniffing each other, and there were even a few cheek rubs. Yes, after nearly a decade of Bhava despising all other felines, she finally had two friends.

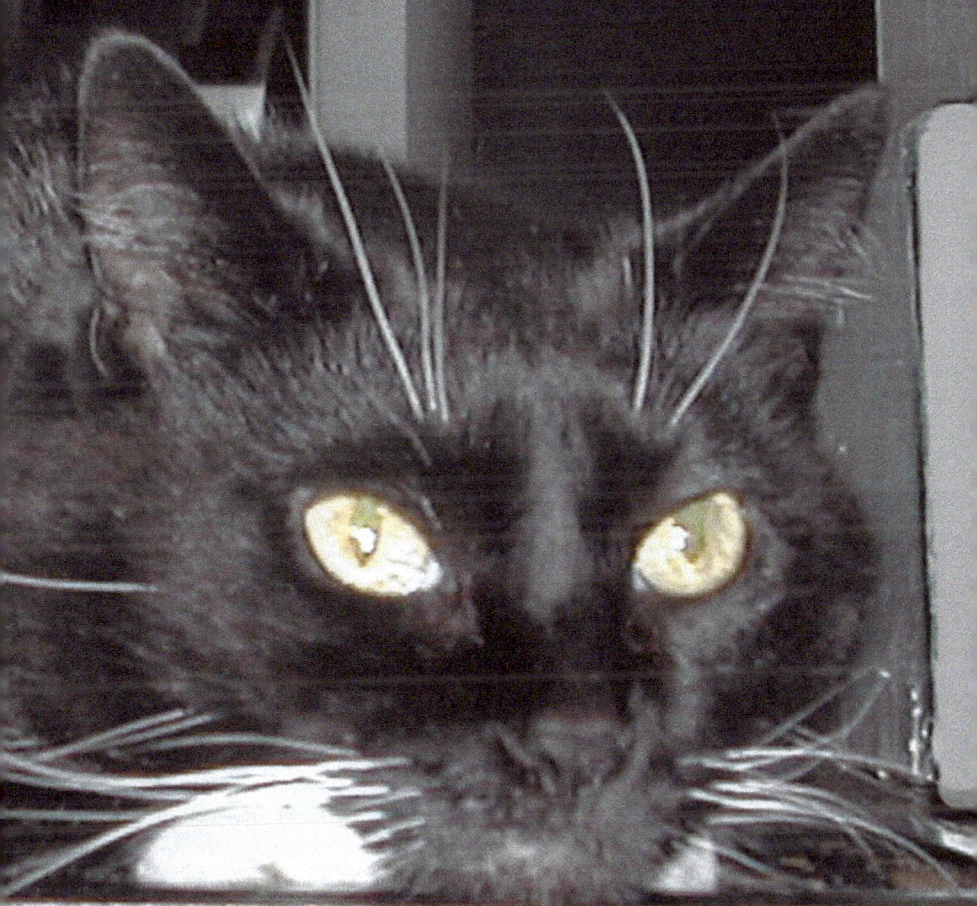

BHAVA ... CONTEMPLATING

ROMEO, SKINNY, AND BHAVA

ROMEO AND SKINNY

Chapter Nine

CONJUGATIONS, CONCLUSIONS, AND CAUTIONS

CONJUGATIONS

(Verb) To SKINNY

Infinitive	To skinny
Past	Skinnied
Present Participle	Skinnying
Past Participle	Skinnied

Present:

I	Skinny
You	Skinny
He, She, It	Skinnies
We	Skinny
You	Skinny
They	Skinny

We should *all* skinny.

FOR EXAMPLE:

- My brother's girlfriend broke up with him last night so I'm going to *skinny* him with tickets to the game tonight.
- I *skinnied* my boss with flowers because she was yelling at everyone yesterday.
- I'm in the process of *skinnying* my not-so-friendly neighbor by sweeping her sidewalk every morning.
- Yesterday, I got *skinnied* when a little boy unexpectedly gave me a big hug for no apparent reason.

CONCLUSIONS

So ... in the ninth chapter, after the ninth inning, but before the hypothetical ninth life of the proverbial cat, I have concluded the following: *The more unlovable someone may seem to be, the more love that particular someone actually needs.*

Skinny reminded me that when others are disquieted, angry, or sad, there is a reason. Most often, it is nothing personal, which makes them easier to *skinny*, but even if it is personal and I happen to be the cause of their anxiety, I can still *skinny* them by taking a big breath and laying down my sword. I have also deduced that I'd better keep an olive tree growing in my metaphorical backyard no matter where I live because I never know when I'm going to need an extra branch. In the bigger picture, does it matter if I'm right about something or not? I mean, who cares ... other than my ego?

No doubt, you have heard the old expression: Patience is its own reward. Well, I have learned that *kindness* is its own reward too. For example, if I take a moment out of a hurried day to say something nice to or just smile at a scowling stranger, there's a good chance that person will walk away feeling a little bit better. And in that moment, when I know I've connected and really *skinnied* someone, it's a palpable emotional lift for me as well, so everybody wins.

No matter what your age or life circumstance, you can *skinny* people (even if you don't speak their language). And obviously you can *skinny* animals too. Never underestimate the power of that wonderful, bright energy. It's contagious and exudes from you and your recipients everywhere you both go. And you know what? They may never forget it. You just don't know when that gesture of kindness is a turning point in someone's day ... or even his or her life. Haven't you had someone say or do something nice that to this day still lingers in the archives of your memory? I bet you do. You can make that kind of imprint on someone else's consciousness, just by following the few simple rules.

RULES AND CAUTIONS
(If You Want to Try Your Hand at *Skinnying*)

Rule 1: Always be authentic. The trick here is to find something genuinely nice. It must be true from your perspective.

Rule 2: Don't give up on anybody ... ever ... but it's okay to take sabbaticals from certain people, to let the seeds of kindness you plant germinate and take root. No matter what you think, no one is immune to *skinnying*.

Rule 3: You can *skinny* anyone, anywhere, anytime, with or without language. Again, sometimes, just a smile can make a huge difference in someone's day. Your job as a *skinnier* is to be on the lookout for those who need to be *skinnied* and *skinny* them in the best way that seems appropriate to you in the moment.

Rule 4: You can't make mistakes. Just be nice, and don't worry about doing it right. Anyone can be a good *skinnier*.

Rule 5: You may find this hard to believe, but ... you can *skinny* yourself. Yes. Right out of a terrible mood. As you develop your *skinnying* skills, certain things will become obvious and appear on your radar that you never noticed before. These become part of your mental vocabulary, part of your *skinnying* repertoire, so to speak. You will naturally begin to see how this can translate to healing hurt feelings or anxious moods in your own day. Don't forget ... all the above rules apply to you as well. Be authentic and don't give up. It doesn't matter where you are or how you do it. And relax. (This bears repeating.) You can't fail. Putting good energy out into the world is a plus no matter what happens.

Okay, so there's always a catch, right? Well, I don't look at it as a catch but rather a caution or reality check. Some people are easier to *skinny* than others (e.g., Sasha versus Bhava). If you are in conflict with someone, this is not necessarily an easy thing to do, especially at first. Your ego is a strong fighter with a loud voice, wants you to be right all the time, and is happy to shout in your ear things like, "It must be someone else's fault," along with other ego-inflated ideas. Well, you'll find a way to work through that once you experience a full *skinny*. Emotionally, it's much lighter on the other side of that ego pull, so as you experience this new, deeply satisfying feeling, you'll be gently lured into trying it again and again until it becomes an automatic response.

As with any new skill, be it playing tennis or a musical instrument, or learning a new language, it gets easier the more you practice, and yes ... it's easier for some than others. Remember a time in your past when you learned a new skill? Think about that feeling you got after you studied and practiced, afraid you were never going to get it. Then you had that breakthrough moment when you realized you weren't thinking intently about how to do it anymore; you were flowing and performing the new skill effortlessly. You'll find that to also be true with *skinnying*. With that in mind, just keep practicing.

You don't have to *skinny* everyone in all situations all at once. Start small. *Skinny* one person a day. (Just think what the world would be like if everyone just *skinnied* one person a day. Wow.) The wonderful thing about Skinny the cat is that he naturally sees the world this way. Instinctively, he's pure love. Evidently, he didn't have to learn it. He is the animal messenger who demonstrated it to us. Perhaps it's not that easy for humans, but it doesn't mean it's impossible. All we can do is to try. Truly, it can only help, not harm.

One last note: With certain people, you may not meet with your desired success with merely one *skinny* or even several consecutive *skinnies*, but remember, the key is to be patient and always keep *skinnying*. Even when you don't get through, you have planted a seed. Make it a commitment. Make it your mission.

It might be moments, days, weeks, months, or even years later, but chances are that seed of kindness and love will eventually sprout and bloom. *Nothing you do is irrelevant.* You can be about love, gentleness, and understanding, or you can be about feeding the anger, the disappointment or negative mood. The choice is yours. Never give up trying ... and stay open. Because someday, when you least expect it, *you* just might *get skinnied* yourself.

EPILOGUE

So, just in case you were wondering: The BACG lives on and is growing. Shortly after I finished the book, an odd-looking black-and-white cat with one blind eye took up residence in the front yard garden, well hidden under the Mexican sage. I have to admit I was a bit frightened by the looks of him; plus, he was quite assertive when I set snacks out on the front porch for the other boys—zooming up to greet me before I even had a chance to set the bowl down. He thought nothing about nosing Skinny or Romeo out of his way to get to those delicious kibble nuggets. He'd take a few furious bites out of one dish, and then dive into the adjacent one to make absolutely sure the same food was in that one too. This two-toned hobo wasn't about to miss a lick. The boys, of course, didn't mind much, but they did have to get used to him (a perfect example that *skinnying* takes a little more time with some than others). But quite frankly, it didn't take long to realize his aggressiveness was due to a simple fact of life. Being the homeless critter he appeared to be, extreme hunger was driving him. And somewhere behind that bullish personality, I had a feeling we would find a soft spot.

Because of the unfortunate but common dilemma in situations such as these, the odd fellow displayed no identification whatsoever. We asked around the neighborhood and put an advertisement in our weekly local rag, *The Argonaut*. Then we made flyers. Or rather, *Robert* made flyers. Staying true to his noble trouper form, Robert got on his bike and rode all over Venice taping and stapling 180 "cat found" flyers on every utility pole in sight.

With no takers and a personality that was growing on us like moss in a damp forest, Robert started referring to him as Mad-Eye for Mad-Eye Moody, one of the characters in the *Harry Potter* series. That quickly morphed into Maddie, which seemed to suit him and us just fine. Robert and I both knew at that point, for all practical purposes, the cat now belonged to us.

Months rolled by, and still, no one showed up to claim the little lost one. Meanwhile, I discovered that beyond the peculiar one-sighted-eye appearance of this ragamuffin nomad (once he felt safe and had his appetite satisfied) was the most lovable temperament imaginable. He had undoubtedly been someone's beloved pet and was used to being cuddled. This was definitely not a feral cat by any means. When I'd pick Maddie up to hold him, he would drop his head down into the crook of my neck and with his purr on high volume, knead his paws into my shoulder and cling to me like a small child. At feeding time, he'd eat ravenously for fifteen seconds or so, and then turn his head to look up at me in pure gratitude. Once eye contact was established, he'd lean his head into my leg as if to say thank you again and then resume wolfing down the chow. By this time, we were under his spell, and I realized that he had *skinnied* all of *us*. (Now, who'd found whose soft spot?)

I bought Maddie a small bed to keep the chill off at night, but Skinny made it his business to break it in. Eventually, the bed sharing expanded, and the next thing we knew, Jan was reporting that she'd caught them all piled up at a nap party over at her place.

So on and on the story goes, but one thing is certain. My world is a much better place since Skinny entered into it. I hope yours is as well.

Love,

Donna

Be sure to visit:

skinnythecat.com

For additional information, email the author at:

skinnythecat@gmail.com

ABOUT THE AUTHOR

In addition to her writing and love of animals, Donna is a voice actor, singer, and songwriter whose songs have appeared in network television shows and major feature films including *Mr. Woodcock, The Bold and the Beautiful, The Unit, The Shield* and *Dawson's Creek,* and is an active member of the Screen Actors Guild, AFTRA, and BMI.

Represented for voice-over by William Morris Endeavor in Beverly Hills, her abundant national commercial credits range from Macy's to United Airlines to Suzuki—just to name a few. Some of the numerous audio book titles she's recorded are: *The Death and Life of American Cities* by Jane Jacobs, Sydney Sheldon's, *Tell Me Your Dreams*; Tami Hoag's, *Taken by Storm*; *Memoirs of Cleopatra* by Margaret George; Laura Zigman's, *Animal Husbandry*; Dana Reinhardt's, *Harmless and Female Intelligence,* by Jane Heller. Donna was also featured as the character *BT* in the premier season of the Japanese anime series *.hack//Sign*.

Originally from the small town of Lancaster, Ohio, the Los Angeles—based writer comes from a family of five musicians and currently resides in Venice Beach, California with her husband, Robert Feist, owner of Ravenswork Studios, along with their seventeen-year old cat, Bhava, newly adopted Maddie, and of course … the rest of those crazy cats.

IN LOVING MEMORY OF MY BELOVED ICHI...

Sweet Sasha...

AND MY PARENTS' CAT, GEORGE: RIP